How To...
save it

How To...
Save it

FIX YOUR FINANCES

BOLA SOL

1 3 5 7 9 10 8 6 4 2

#Merky Books
20 Vauxhall Bridge Road
London SW1V 2SA

#Merky Books is part of the Penguin Random House group of companies
whose addresses can be found at global.penguinrandomhouse.com.

Penguin
Random House
UK

First published in the United Kingdom by #Merky Books in 2021

www.penguin.co.uk

A CIP catalogue record for this book is available from the British Library.

ISBN 9781529118810

Text design © Andreas Brooks
Set in 10/13 pt Source Serif Variable Roman
Typeset by Jouve (UK), Milton Keynes
Printed and bound in Great Britain by Clays Ltd, Elcograf S.p.A.

The authorised representative in the EEA is Penguin Random House Ireland,
Morrison Chambers, 32 Nassau Street, Dublin D02 YH68

Penguin Random House is committed to a sustainable future
for our business, our readers and our planet. This book is made from
Forest Stewardship Council® certified paper.

MIX
Paper from
responsible sources
FSC
www.fsc.org   FSC® C018179

CONTENTS

FOREWORD

Millions of us go through life knowing we should do more to save and invest for the future, but we leave it at the bottom of our to-do lists because we don't know where to start. This isn't surprising given most of us weren't taught how to save and invest at school, the investment industry was built to serve only a wealthy few, and banks often seem more interested in selling us products than helping us to achieve our financial goals.

This all means that our money isn't working as hard for us as it should. And it's the reason why Moneybox came to life.

Our co-founders, school friends Ben and Charlie, were chatting over a drink in the pub one evening, discussing why so few of us have access to the tools and information we need to make the most of our money. We're faced with so many daunting questions, but we aren't armed with the knowledge to answer them. What is an interest rate? When should I start saving for my retirement, and what makes a good pension provider? Are stocks and shares safe? What is an ISA? How do I create a savings budget, and stick to it? It all becomes completely overwhelming, especially if you don't know who to turn to for answers, or perhaps you are too embarrassed to ask.

The biggest challenge seems to be taking the first step. The thing is, for most of us, our first jobs won't yield a six-figure salary allowing us to put away a big lump sum for the future every month. Rather, our first pay cheques are likely to be eaten up by bills, eye-watering rent and student loan repayments, making anything we do manage to save a small victory in itself. We all feel the pressure to do the right thing with what we earn, but many of us feel we don't have enough left at the end of the month to even bother. There are many other factors, from our childhood experiences through to our access to education, that can also affect our relationship with money.

We believe that everyone should have access to the tools, information and encouragement they need to achieve their financial potential, and that starting early, however small, can make a huge difference.

When we launched Moneybox, we were committed to making saving and investing available to everyone. We made it possible to open an account with as little as £1, and to invest the spare change from your everyday purchases using round-ups. We wanted to encourage people to get started and show them ways to save without thinking too much about it. Our entire service was built around being easy to use, friendly, engaging and, most importantly, jargon-free.

In the last four years, we've helped more than half a million people save and invest for their future, and for us this is just the beginning.

Here are five things to keep in mind on your financial journey:

1. It may sound clichéd, but saving is more like a marathon than a sprint. Your current financial situation is just your starting point, and success is based on building sustainable habits rather than making radical short-term promises to yourself that you won't be able to keep. Having a clear view of your short-, medium-, and long-term goals is a great place to start.

2. Give yourself a break. You don't actually need to be a financial expert to make the most of your money, and you shouldn't be afraid to talk about money with your friends, or ask for help. However small or stupid you may think that question is – ask it, because you and only you have the power to take care of your financial future (and other people might be wondering the same thing!).

3. Even though the world of personal finance might seem daunting, the great news is that once you know what you're looking for, there are some fantastic tools and products out there that are designed to help you save for your future. Improvements in technology have meant that apps like ours have broken down the barriers to entry more than ever before.

4. Let go of the idea of being perfect, or thinking you're behind. There is no perfect time to start saving. Just start now, however small the amount, and focus on the future.

5. Lastly, whether you're saving for a holiday, a new car, your first home or your wedding, it's important to celebrate every milestone as you get closer to reaching your goal, regardless of how often you save or how much.

We hope this book will give you the motivation to get started – just picking it up means you're already on the right path. So, happy saving and investing, and safe travels on the financial journey you are about to embark on – you'll be amazed by what you can achieve once you take the first step.

Team Moneybox

iNTRODUCTION

WHY SHOULD WE SAVE?

The word 'save' has always had a positive association – there's an element of hope in those four little letters. Whether it's to save someone's life, to keep someone safe, or even to 'save the best till last'. It's forward focused. However, when we attach that word to *money*, it starts to feel like that thing on our 'to do' list we promised to come back to when we had the time.

If 2020 has taught us anything, though, it's that we all need to pay attention to our finances and have a viable financial back-up plan. With things like furloughs, unexpected redundancies and universal credit hovering in the wings, we cannot and should not be attempting to survive purely off what our monthly income happens to be. We need to make a concerted effort to think about our financial future, to start planning and then take action to make it better.

Getting your finances in order is not going to be an overnight success story, but nor will it be a solo mission. Wherever you are in life, you are not alone in this, and the ability to save is not for one group of people from a privileged background. Getting your finances in order is a journey, one I believe we can all embark on, with the help of a few tips that I hope to provide. But be warned: it's a journey where doubts may side-track you, and you may even fundamentally question your ability to reach some of the financial goals you've set. You'll also think deeply about whether your bank balance is for or against you, and you'll always have that one bill that's due soon or maybe even past due. However, in the end, you'll be grateful for the journey, as it will help you to understand your money and the lessons you possibly didn't even know you needed to learn.

WHO AM I?

In essence, I've spent at least two decades infatuated with numbers. When I was younger, I would watch the TV programme *Countdown* every afternoon without fail, because I was obsessed with how numbers worked. Since then, I have made it my priority to break down numbers and make the understanding of them accessible, in the hope that, through my efforts, other people can experience the same joy I get when a particular formula works, or simply, when numbers make sense. Over the last five years, I've been privileged to work with some of the biggest brands in the world in order to help them and their employees grapple with their finances. Some of the companies I've worked with include Puma, *gal-dem*, the *Financial Times*, Sky News, the Royal Bank of Scotland and NatWest, and I've been featured on and in GUAP, BBC, *Forbes*, *Stylist*, Black Ballad and Refinery 29.

When I completed my degree in Mathematics and Finance at the University of Essex in 2014, I felt it was so unfair that only a select group of people like me and my fellow graduates had access to knowledge that, to my mind, should not only be free for everyone but would financially empower them too. Plus, it was brought to my attention again and again, the more brands I worked with and the higher up I went, how few people I came across had my background – black, first generation, working class – and that bugged me. It felt even more of a stark contrast whenever I talked to my peers about money matters, such as when I'd casually mention a simple term like 'investment' and see their eyes glaze over. This made me think that a fundamental lack of understanding re personal finances was not only a widespread problem, but there was maybe space for a new conversation, and for education regarding money generally that really brought more people in.

So, in 2015, I started my own company, Refined Currency. The aim was to provide people with a place to learn about finance in a format that skipped all the jargon in the hope that some terminologies would become demystified. And, alongside all this, I continued to work full time in finance and banking, which was a pretty challenging juggle. However, increasingly, finding a solution to bridge these two worlds became a focal point for me.

WHY WE NEED A BOOK ABOUT MONEY

So often, I doubt myself and ask whether I am the right person to be speaking so confidently about money. Unlike many who speak about this stuff, I am one of six children born to a single mother from South London. I've struggled with money, I've thrived with it, and it's given me adrenaline rushes as well as major anxiety. Yet, from having my card declined in college when I went to buy a Snickers bar to being given a budget of £10,000 to manage as President of the Student Union at Richmond College, money continues to teach me that abundance is a mindset.

Moreover, the many conversations I've had with people over the years have repeatedly reminded me that one size does not fit all when it comes to our financial circumstances. My personal and professional relationship with money, and my particular background, has enabled me to give practical advice, as well as spread faith that if *I* can get my money in order, so can *you*.

I have written this book in order to help you to change the way you think about your money. From the habits you formed years ago to the habits you have now, all your experiences with your finances are shaping you, just as they've shaped me.

Coming from a mother and father who were born in Nigeria, I was always told to study hard and get a good job, in the hope I'd make enough money to live a good life. But, as time passed, house prices became ever more expensive, recession(s) hit, Nando's stopped giving you change for a tenner, and it felt like there wasn't much spare change left to put into the piggy bank. So I've had to take what my parents taught me and adapt it to the world I live in *now*.

Everywhere I look, assumptions and presumptions continue to be made about what saving is, and who has the power to save. There's a lot to unpack, but I'm here to tell you/show you that saving and investments aren't only for the corporate CEO types on a six-figure salary, or that saving can only be achieved if you hide your money under your mattress. This book is here to show that saving is for *everyone*, including *you*.

WHAT YOU'LL FIND IN THIS BOOK

1. A reminder not to compare your financial journey to that of others.

2. How to separate who you are from what you earn.

3. The best way to make decisions about purchases once you understand the minor and major differences between debt and credit.

4. Figuring out the best way to budget for you.

5. Knowing how to make, and think about, short-term, mid-term and long-term goals.

CHAPTER I

MINDSET

When it comes to money, our beliefs and mindset are everything. For example, do you believe you can be financially stable, rich even, despite your upbringing? Or do you self-sabotage? When you have money troubles, do you bury your head in the sand or do you face the problem head-on and accept the challenge? The way we behave and what we think about money is key to building the financial success we want.

OUR UPBRINGING AND MONEY

Our relationship with money starts at home, and it's important to assess how your childhood correlates to how you spend and save your money today.

As a child, I never understood how important money was until I saw my mother cry when she was making us all dinner one evening. She couldn't hold back her tears and my brother put his arm around her to console her and she collapsed into his arms. Seeing the woman I regarded as a superhero break down was a powerful shock and a reminder that even the strongest characters in your life are human. At the time this happened, I was ten years old, and it took that moment and a sequence of others for me to identify that we were struggling financially, as I'd been oblivious. In my innocence, I offered my mother my own pocket money when she had finished wiping her tears, and she laughed. What we didn't have in finances we made up for in love, but from that point onwards, I wanted to make our financial situation better so that, as a family, we could laugh a lot more than we cried.

THE COMPARISON GAME

Living in a society that encourages us to constantly look at what others are doing, that pushes the idea that being successful is everything, it is all too easy to question our own intrinsic value without taking into consideration how much our race, class, gender or social status impacts our net worth. Look at contemporary music culture and how much it glorifies numbers and riches. Look at the corporate world and the concentration of power and status. Look at Hollywood and what is considered fame and fortune. We become our own worst enemy when we try to compare our own value to the constantly shifting societal standard. We are so much more than our bank balance.

LIMITING BELIEFS

Perhaps the hardest part of overcoming the limiting beliefs that hold so many of us back may be acknowledging that they exist in the first place. You may have carried them around with you for so long that you don't even realise that you could be sabotaging yourself. And yet, I wholeheartedly believe that everything we speak into our lives matters and can come to fruition. Let me explain. Remember the childhood taunt 'Sticks and stones may break my bones but words will never hurt me'? That may have carried less significance/been easy to brush off when we were younger, but, with the rise of social media, what we comment on, double-tap or co-sign with emojis matters, and can have both positive as well as detrimental knock-on effects.

It's the same with money. How many times have you heard or said the following or similar?

— 'We can't afford it because we are poor.'

— 'I couldn't trust myself with that amount of money.'

— 'Someone else would be better for the job.'

— 'I don't know/don't think I can ask for a pay rise.'

Bad habits can take a while to change for the better. We all have habits that we reinforce every day, every week, every year, and some are for the good and some are not. In fact, research shows that, once we have acknowledged a bad habit and set about changing, it can take eighteen days and upwards to break a habit.* That gives you a lot of opportunities to fail. But here are some tips to get you through the initial stages:

1. **GIVE YOURSELF A GRACE PERIOD** – No one gets anything perfect on the first go, or even the

---

* www.sciencealert.com/how-long-it-takes-to-break-a-habit-according-to-science

second or third. Changing habits takes time, as it's all about changing your mental stimuli.

2. **RECORD WHAT YOU'RE PLANNING TO CHANGE** – No matter how far technology advances, nothing beats writing stuff down with paper and pen. It doesn't have to be a long, elaborate piece of work. It can be one sentence. Once you've done that, stick it somewhere you can see it. Visual reminders of your goals can be helpful.

3. **GET TO THE HEART OF THE MATTER** – Only you know why certain habits truly exist in your life. Are you willing to go with your why? Explore your motivations. It may not only save you money, it may open up more room for change.

YOUR MONEY MINDSET

Mindset is everything. Here are three handy ways to stop yourself from hindering your own progress:

1. When a negative thought creeps up on you, identify it and change it to a positive one. This won't always be easy, especially at first, because past mistakes may try to add weight and drag you

down, but shake it off, take a deep breath and move your mind forward. 'I'm broke' is a common example.

I can't reiterate enough that using the term 'I'm broke', even as a joke, is very damaging to your money mindset. When we tell ourselves we are broke, it sounds like an irreversible condition, and that is simply not the case.

Change your wording from 'I'm broke' to 'I'm having a temporary cash-flow problem, I'll be back up in a minute' or 'I'm currently a bit low on funds'. It sounds like a small thing, but it makes a difference. Whatever situation you are in financially isn't permanent, so ensure you don't speak like it is. Trust me, your subconscious will thank you for this variation in wording.

2. Stop telling yourself that everyone is better at money than you are. We are all human and we are all learning how to improve. That journey of improvement takes time so be sure to tell yourself you are progressing positively.

3. Use positive affirmations. I used to think these were incredibly corny and only for highly

'spiritual' kinds of people, but I'm here to tell you they work. At the lowest points of my life, I would recite positive affirmations on my way to work. For example, 'I'm smart, I'm kind, I'm capable', and so many other similar phrases, work a treat on good *and* bad days. Hype yourself up. You're worth it. Be sure to get out of the habit of using statements such as, 'I'm bad with money.' This is a phrase I constantly hear people use to describe themselves, as if their aptitude with money is something fixed that they were born with, like the colour of their eyes, when actually it's a self-fulfilling prophecy. Your financial future is worth so much more than the circumstances you grew up in. You are *not* bad with money, you are *getting better* with money, as a result of your past experiences. Learn not to beat yourself up about the things you cannot change. So, as often as you can, switch 'I'm bad with money' into 'I am getting better with my finances every day'. We are constantly learning and growing, so give yourself permission to evolve without harsh judgement.

Since we are on the topic of limiting beliefs and the damage they can do, I want to bring up the topic of

Covid-19. As 2020 progressed, it seemed like, one day at a time, the walls were closing in. The news went from bad to worse for everyone, and it felt as if there was no escape. On at least two different occasions, I had what felt like nervous breakdowns, involving panic attacks. It was dark. Between Black Lives Matter, George Floyd, Breonna Taylor and Belly Mujinga, as well as the pandemic, I couldn't hear myself think, let alone feel myself breathe. To add insult to injury, I lost my day job and I was the highest earner in a house of five. While no one depended on my income, I felt a weight that was indescribable, because I so badly didn't want my mum to have to go to work. I was told I'd lost my job a week before the second anniversary of my dad's passing. We also lost people in our extended family through Covid-19 and I just couldn't fake positive vibes anymore. I was crumbling. The only thing that kept me sane during this time was the prayers of my loved ones.

This year has been particularly bad for many of us, but there will always be times in your life when it feels as if the world is closing in and the repercussions may well be more than just financial. At such moments, you need to call on your support system because they will give you the affirmations you need when you don't have the capacity. There have probably been countless times when you have been the person that other people have leaned on. Remember that it's okay for you to do the leaning as well. No person is an island, and that saying should be reflected in every area of your life.

LEARN TO SAY 'NO'

Every invitation you receive does not need to be accepted. Equally, just because you have the money available, it doesn't mean that you need to spend it. I find we speak a lot in monetary terms, but we do not speak enough in energy and time terms, which are just as important to consider.

Opportunity cost represents the potential benefits an individual, investor or business misses out on when choosing one alternative over another. The idea of opportunity cost is a major concept in economics.* My fairy godmother (and everyone else's too), Oprah Winfrey, once said that 'no is a complete sentence'. Get out of the habit of feeling the need to explain yourself to people past a level you care to. When you are making financial decisions, you are usually

* www.investopedia.com/terms/o/opportunitycost.

making them by yourself or with your loved ones. So, think about who you decide to give explanations to. Learn to say no without feeling guilty.

QUESTION EVERYTHING

So often we don't value ourselves enough and we forget how much value we add not only to our lives but to other people's. It is imperative that you see the necessity in what you are not only doing but what you are being. It is possible to be both humble and confident: this is exactly what is needed in every negotiation of your life. Balance is key. Let's not just take what is simply handed to us; let's question whether or not the negotiator also sees the value and let's not be afraid to walk away in the event that they don't.

1. **BE MINDFUL OF WHAT IS BEING ADVERTISED** – Growing up, we were all taught to look both ways before we cross the road. Now it's time that we become mindful of the content we are consuming. Our mobile phones have turned into mini-laptops and all forms of advertising are available on our devices. Every company has an e-commerce store of some kind and there is an ad at every turn. Think about what

you are letting occupy your mind and spirit. Advertisers know how to burrow into your brain without you even realising it.

2. **CHANGE LOCATION** – As shopping centres continue to dominate our cities and lives, we have to consider how we utilise them. When meeting friends, to consider how whether it's actually a good idea to meet in a shopping centre where there are multiple stores to attract you. Instead of visiting these places with friends, try going for a coffee in the park or cooking dinner, going for a walk, jog or run with loved ones, and, of course, when the weather permits, going for a picnic instead.

3. **CARRY CASH** – There have been countless times when I have felt compelled to go into a shop and spend money I hadn't anticipated spending, and the best way I have found to overcome this urge is by knowing that I don't have cards available. While I appreciate contactless payment via my smartphone is also an option, I make it a point not to carry devices on me when out and about, so contactless isn't available. Ask yourself, is this a method that might work for you, or some variation of it?

EMOTIONAL SPENDING TRIGGERS

Between paying for things like rent, phone bills, travel and other stuff that crops up, life can be expensive. Take notice of your day-to-day spending. So often we find ourselves spending in such a routine way that we disassociate the emotional connection attached. However, at times, your emotions can trigger you into spending too much money, and it's important to be conscious of when it's happening. Quite often, emotional spending can derail all your saving plans.

There are various emotions that lead us to spend way too much money. Now is the time to learn what causes *you* to spend in a way that derails your attempts to gain control of your finances.

Personally speaking, my menstrual cycle makes me spend too much money. Premenstrual syndrome (PMS) is the medical term for the symptoms women often experience in the weeks before their period. In my case, PMS messes with all my hormones to the point where I begin eating anything and spending everything that is spare. The keyword here is 'spare'. When I am triggered, I find myself online shopping at 1 a.m., because, in my mind, I think I have no clothes, yet when I wake up in the morning and open my wardrobe, I, of course, find that I do. And then it dawns on me that I've been on an emotionally triggered shopping spree and I roll my eyes at myself as I contact retailers to cancel orders.

Another emotional trigger can be experiencing a breakup of any kind. Whether it is a friendship or a relationship, this can potentially have an adverse effect on your finances. There is an all-too-tempting impulse to somehow prove that you are doing *just fine* while trying to move on from the hurt, whether privately or for all the world to see. This can result in feeling the need to eat more or buy too many items in the hope that you can magically feel like you've started again and the pain will have vanished.

BARGAINS

Pricing is a pretty psychological business. Many brands use the concept of '99', e.g. 99p or £99.99, to make the price sound a lot less than it is, but we must not be penny wise and pound foolish. You need to ensure you focus on what you are spending instead of what the very rich retailer is telling you that you are 'saving'. I often tell myself that these big shops have their money, so make sure you have yours too.

RETAIL THERAPY

'Get in loser, we're going shopping.'

Clueless.

Whether you're having a great day, a bad one, or you got the best news of your life, a clothing store is always there to make you feel like you just won the lottery. As someone who has fallen into this trap many times over the years, I am here to tell you that the high is temporary and your problems will still be waiting for you after you've paid for your goods. A great hack I've found to curb my shopping habit is to window shop or put whatever you want in your virtual online shopping basket and then, most importantly, leave it there. When your next payday arrives, only then see if the items are still there and if you still want them. I bet, more often than not, they've lost their initial appeal.

TIP

A rule of thumb I use whenever I go shopping is to eat beforehand. Also, make a list so you aren't tempted to spend beyond the limit you set.

KEEP GOING

My story is not dissimilar from other working-class, first-generation kids. Quite often, our mothers were and still are the backbone and breadwinners of our families. Their work ethic is instilled in us, and the importance of persevering instead of quitting was always hammered home, something we should learn to apply to money too. I remember telling my mother I 'couldn't be bothered' to complete something, and immediately she told it to me straight: 'You don't stop what you started until you are finished.' No messing. I was shocked that my decision had made her react so strongly, but it was a great lesson. The key message here is that one financial blip doesn't mean your whole world falls down. Even if you fall down financially seven times, stand right on up for the eighth time. Keep going.

CHAPTER 2

BUDGET

START AT THE BEGINNING

I often find that people don't want to talk about the reality of budgeting. They're a bit embarrassed about not knowing how. It is okay to admit if you have never budgeted before, but, now you have this book, let me tell you – you need to start.

While budgeting may seem like a mundane task, it is vital if you want to improve your financial circumstances. Essentially, unless you can see where your money is coming from and where your money is going to, you won't get anywhere. So often people say 'Where did all my money go?' You can give yourself a more accurate answer when you start taking budgeting seriously.

Budgeting effectively allows you to figure out where you are forming bad habits, what you are prioritising in your spending, and where you can potentially save more. The importance of budgeting is knowing it's not a one-time exercise, because every month is different, and it should be treated as such. It has to accurately and realistically reflect your personal financial incomings and outgoings. There's no point trying to kid yourself.

Budgeting begins with getting cosy with your finances, and by the end of this chapter I hope you will feel comfortable enough to sit down with your payslip and give it a go.

CHOOSE A METHOD

You have to budget in a way that feels natural to you if you want it to work. Choose a method that will keep you on track and hold you accountable. Which of the following feels the most natural to you?

— Spreadsheets

— Pen and paper

— Apps

— Envelopes

> **TIP**
>
> The envelope method helps you categorise your money for a certain period of time, usually week by week. Examples of categories include groceries, entertainment and travel. There is no limit to how many categories you

can have, however keep it to about 3–5 so that you are not carrying too much cash around.

The envelope system is extremely beneficial, especially if you are new to budgeting and managing your money.

— If you are a visual person, the envelope method can help you see how much you spend. It may assist you in spending less because you can see where the money is going.

— Discipline and focus play a large role in the management of the envelope system as you need to make sure that you don't overspend. This is a great way to develop better self-control with your finances.

CONSISTENCY AND TRANSPARENCY

I'm not here to lie to you – budgeting can be boring. I love numbers and yet I detest budgeting and every form of admin available, but I always remember what I told myself growing up: I need to be able to see for myself where my money is going. When Rihanna sang 'Bitch Better Have My Money', it was because her own accountant tried to play her. If it can happen to her, it can happen to you. Do *not* let anyone play with your livelihood. Budgeting every month is essential in order to know what is happening with your finances. No one should be able to steal what you have rightfully earned, but you will never know what's missing if you don't check up on what is yours.

COMING BACK FROM A SPLURGE

Man cannot live on bread alone, but when you screw up your finances, bread may be all you have. For example, I have lived on Indomie – a brand of Indonesian noodles – before now. Not by choice but because I had to.

We've all been there, haven't we? You've spent too much and it has ruined your budget, if you even had one to begin with. But the good thing about having a budgeting method, and creating that habit as a regular thing, is that you can always start again from wherever you find yourself.

Here are three ways you can get your budget back on track after you've gone over:

1. **CHECK WHAT YOU'VE BOUGHT** – One useful tip is to keep tags on items you haven't worn or used until you're completely sure that you want them. You'd be surprised how grateful you are for that extra £50 when you realise the money is more important than the outfit you felt was essential at the time. After all, you were 'worth it' before L'Oréal made it a catchphrase. Keep your receipts, don't pop all the tags, and when you run a little low, don't be afraid to return things and reclaim that money.

2. **DON'T USE MORE CREDIT** – When you feel like your bank account is in meltdown, please do not look to that piece of plastic. For those who have a credit card, you'll know the emotional rollercoaster it can put you on. What can feel like an adrenaline rush can rapidly lead to the feeling of nausea when you have to pay what you owe, *plus* APR. And don't forget the APR includes not only the interest on the credit that's been extended to you, but also all fees and other costs involved in obtaining the loan, as that is essentially what a credit card is. We will get into

all this in more depth later, but since we are on the topic of credit, I'd also suggest you don't use an overdraft unless the odds are truly in your favour, and, even then, only in an emergency. The odds being in your favour means the overdraft is at 0% interest and you have a plan of action about how you're going to pay it back.

3. **SET UP A MISCELLANEOUS FUND** – Ideally, there should be a section in your budget for circumstances you didn't anticipate happening. Every month, set some money aside to act as a buffer if anything goes wrong. It's important to establish that this is very different from an emergency fund. This is similar to finding a tenner in your jeans pocket. It's the surprise present you buy for yourself even though you know what it is.

THE 50/30/20 RULE

People often ask me how they should divide their money and I always say it is completely up to the individual. However, there is a famous rule called the 50/30/20 rule. The way I remember it is by giving it the acronym 'NWS'. NWS stands for *needs*, *wants* and *savings*. As we've discussed earlier and will again throughout this book, it is up to you to define what is a need and what is a want in your life. But, so help me God, you *must* make it a rule of life to save. Yes, 20% may not always be feasible each and every month, but it is absolutely vital that saving becomes part of your everyday experience. Your future self will thank you.

BUDGETING APPS

As the world continues to become increasingly high tech, it is important that you realise that there are so many tools out there, many of them free, that you can use to help you budget. Drop the excuses, pick up your phone and go check out some apps! Here is my own list of recommended budgeting apps, but there are more every day.

— **MONEY DASHBOARD** – A free online personal financial management service that shows you all of your online financial accounts in one place. It categorises and analyses all of your transactions to help you understand how to make your money work for you.

— **YNAB** – You Need a Budget makes it simple to access your financial information in real time and you can share this with a partner too. You can set goals together and see your financial data in the format of graphs.

— **MINT** – One of the great features of Mint is that you can check your credit score as many times as you like and it also gives you tips on how to improve it. Mint is a great app with which to see all of your money in one place and keep an eye on your credit too.

— **EMMA** –If you get confused by all the different outgoings you have, Emma syncs your budget to payday which can allow you to get a better insight into your spending behaviour. In addition to budgeting, you can track and cancel any subscriptions that you currently don't find useful.

— **CLEO** – Cleo gives a personal feel to money management. It's like texting a friend who will tell you the truth about your financial situation. Texts can include messages such as, 'Can I afford to have a pizza tonight?' Plus, it uses memes so you can have a laugh at your screen while staying in the know with your finances.

A BUDGET BREAKDOWN

At the risk of stating the obvious, whatever method
you use, the first thing to look at when you are doing
your budget is your income. There are so many
ways in which money comes to us, and it's important
that we account for every single form without taking
it for granted, regardless of how big or small the
amount is.

Here are some examples of sources of income:

— Salary

— Freelance Work

— Dividends

— Returns

- Bonus
- Interest
- Universal Credit

FIXED EXPENSES

Now, let's get into your fixed expenses. These are outgoings that don't tend to fluctuate over time. For example: rent, insurance, any subscriptions you may have, any leases you may have, or any other set payments, such as a phone bill, internet bill, and so on. These are non-negotiable, as a rule.

VARIABLE EXPENSES

Next, let's get into the variable expenses. This is an area that can be pretty volatile because our variable expenses can fluctuate according to our lifestyle at any particular point in time. Here are some examples of my variable expenses to give you an idea. Some vary month to month, some only crop up once or twice a year.

- Credit Card (monthly repayment)
- DVLA

- Online Shopping

- Therapy

- Overdraft Expenses

- Amazon Prime (monthly/annually)

- Clothes

- Beauty Costs

- Hair Costs

- Travel

SAVINGS

Now you should have a section for your savings. And there are many different types of savings, from an emergency fund to an individual savings account (ISA) and much more. First, you need to figure out what you class as short-term savings goals and what are maybe more long-term ones. Short-term can be as little as a few months, so shall we say twelve months or less? A medium-term goal, meanwhile, would be anything between one and three years, and a long-term goal would be three to five years or more. This is very dependent on who you're talking to, though, as some people may define long-term goals as a ten-year-plus plan. As I said, it is up to you to define the duration you set for your short-term, medium-term and long-term goals.

GIFTS

Then, towards the end of my budget, I have a section labelled 'charity and gifts'. In this section I have pay it forward, charitable donations and religious donations. Every month I decide to give away a portion of my earnings based on what I feel I can afford, as that's important to me. However, I can't stress enough the importance of not allowing yourself to be pressured by external forces about whether you choose to give away some of your money. As we discussed earlier, no two months are the same with budgeting, so there shouldn't be a single entity telling you where to put your money on a consistent basis. Especially as you are the only person getting up and going to work to get that money.

MISCELLANEOUS

Last but not least, we have the miscellaneous section. A miscellaneous section and miscellaneous fund are two different things, of course. An example of things that can go in the miscellaneous section are bank fees that you forget are adding up in your account, or maybe postage fees. The thing we can do with money at times is tell ourselves that the little costs aren't as important, but whether it's £3 here or £1.98 there, it all adds up, and I need you to factor it into your budget. In regards to a miscellaneous fund, I like to keep £50–£150 spare for circumstances I didn't see coming, like a parking fine or sometimes it can simply be me going over my budget.

PREDICTING THE FUTURE

Something I remind my clients about regularly is that a budget is a forecast. When they tell you the weather, they say this is what it's forecast to be, and we all know we sometimes go outside and find that that is not the case. The same goes for a budget. The whole point of a budget is that you are able to forecast where your finances should go, but it pays to have some room for slippage. Make sure you refer back to your budget at the end of that month and see if you have gone over or under and why. Money is always coming and going, but the whole point of a budget is that you can physically see the difference. You get to call yourself out and say, 'I need to know what I'm spending in a particular area of my life.'

NEEDS AND WANTS

We can all agree that our needs are easy to identify. We need a roof over our heads, clothes on our back, food, electricity, gas, water, et cetera, et cetera. This is what we can call the basic survival kit. Where budgeting gets tricky is when wants come into it. Our mind has this habit of telling us that the things we *want* should go on the *need* list as well. The older I get, the more I tell myself that I *need* particular things, such as getting my eyebrows done, getting my eyelashes done, getting my hair done every month, having a gym membership, going to the chiropractor ... the list can go on and on. While there is nothing wrong with any of the things I've mentioned, when it comes to your finances, there has to be a priority list in your mind about what needs to come first.

Everywhere, whether it's on Twitter or other social media or in real life, I hear the endless refrain of 'I need that.' But when you keep creating this ever growing list of things that you supposedly need, bear in mind that you could subconsciously create more anxiety around how much money you should be making in order to fulfil a particular lifestyle.

39

When your income goes up, don't upgrade your lifestyle, upgrade your life instead. This could be anything – from saving for a mortgage to buying a property outside of London or going on holiday or buying that phone you've wanted for a long time. Achieving these more substantial goals may mean holding off on your more superficial needs – which are really wants – for a while, but the end result will be so much more.

CREATING A 'FUN FUND'

Growing up, money wasn't something that represented joy for me. It represented greed, incessant bills, and, I'm sad to say, kept my loved ones fighting over inheritance money. They say it's power that corrupts, but I believe a lot of that starts with money. But while money gets a bad reputation, and I can see why, it can also bring a lot of good into people's lives. I'll give you an example. I once got my friend tickets to London Fashion Week for her birthday because she wanted to work in fashion, although she studied psychology at university. She now works in fashion doing a job she really loves. Of course, she doesn't owe her career to me, far from it, but every experience helps, and I like to think my gift made a difference. Money doesn't buy you happiness, but knowing it can make someone's face light up is always a motivation. For all the hours you put in, for all the research you do, for all the time you invest into every form of education possible, for all the conversations you have, you deserve to have fun with your money. Yes! Newsflash: money isn't only for bills; it's for fun too. Every time you get paid, make sure that you create a section in your budget so you can do something you enjoy, because it's important that we remember to live, love and laugh with intention.

ACCOUNT FOR CELEBRATIONS

Think about all the friends you have; think about how much you love them and how much you want to support them in their individual life journeys. It's beautiful, isn't it? To see your friends blossom. Be sure to account for how their blossoming happiness also costs you a tiny fortune, however. Please note that this will all be worth it and, in the moments of joy, you will forget the cost, but it's still worth being pragmatic and factoring it in. Personally, I tend to give my friends and family a rest on my birthday, so I usually have what we call a 'rice at a home' party. In my culture, rice is a staple. There is rice and stew, there is jollof rice, fried rice, and so many other delectable styles. As I've gotten older, I've also learned to love pilau rice, Singapore fried rice, chicken fried rice, and many more. In fact, I'm going to stop talking about rice because I'm getting hungry.

My point is, life is to be celebrated and it's important to think about who you are willing to put your money behind. In this life there will always be people that you will fall out with or who pass out of your life, but be sure not to regret the finances you put behind that person along with the energy you gave them. In the moment it was worth it, so allow that moment to continue without resenting what it was. Every time I say congratulations to a loved one, I do question what it's going to cost me. I have no problem spending my money on loved ones, but it's important to know exactly how much that love is going to cost me so I can be prepared.

CHAPTER 3

save

AUDITING WHAT YOU HAVE

It can be a painful wake-up call seeing what you are spending your money on. However, there comes a time when we all need to do an audit of our personal finances. That means checking through transactions from all of your accounts so you can see exactly where your money is going. To do this, you'll need to check the following:

— The account you pay your salary into

— Any credit card(s) you may have

— Any other account(s) you have

There are a few regular culprits that can account for where your money goes. In my experience, it's typically food and drink related – a brunch here, a birthday dinner there, a random meet-up here, a drink there, and so on.

CATEGORISE YOUR TRANSACTIONS

Assuming you do online and mobile banking, many major banks give you the option to label your spending into set categories, such as:

- Transport
- Groceries
- Eating Out
- Gas Bill
- Electric Bill
- Entertainment
- Holidays
- Shopping
- Family
- Personal Care

With some banks, you can even create your own categories.

When saving truly becomes a priority in your life, the first thing you're going to do is look at all of these categories and decide which ones have to be cut back. Remember, this doesn't mean that you have to go cold turkey on any of the things that you love. What it *does* mean is that you have to be more sensible in order to achieve your savings goals.

CASHBACK

Cashback often refers to one of two financial transactions related to credit and debit cards. When you use a credit card with cashback rewards, the cardholder will receive a small percentage of the amount spent on each purchase. This encourages you to spend on your credit card, so ensure you do so with discipline. Debit card cashback (also known as 'cash out' in Australia and New Zealand), meanwhile, is a service offered to retail customers whereby an amount is added to the total purchase price of a transaction paid by debit card and the customer receives that amount in cash along with the purchase. Convenient, but not the added bonus that credit cashback is.

TIP

It's important to remember that there are also cashback websites, which pay a percentage of money when members purchase goods and services via the affiliate links. Currently, I get a percentage back on anything I spend via

---

Amazon because I am part of the Amazon affiliate scheme. I used to find all of those adverts on YouTube really annoying – when people would say, 'Guess how much I make on Amazon,' and I used to just think you're a liar – however I'm here to tell you that cashback is the truth and people talking about Amazon affiliate schemes are actually right.

REWARD SCHEMES

While slightly different from cashback, it's really important to be part of a reward scheme for all the places you shop at regularly. Whenever I shop at Marks & Spencer, Sainsbury's and Tesco, or have a cheeky Nando's, I always make sure that I have my reward cards on me. In fact, my favourite thing to do is to collect my friends' points after I have told them so many times to get a card and they have failed to do so. The future is reward systems, and you need to get on it. Ask your friends where they shop and tell them to join the reward system.

DISCOUNTS

Wherever possible, make sure you ask for a discount. Let's face it, I am never ever going to say I wish I'd paid full price at Selfridges, am I? Between us, my friends and I are always looking for a discount and there is no shame in it.

Here are four ways you can ask for a discount:

1. **GOOGLE IT** – Whenever I go into a store or restaurant, one of the first things I do is Google their name and the word 'discounts' on my phone, to see what comes up – sometimes it works, sometimes it doesn't. Then I go over to the lovely salesperson with my best smile, greet them (acknowledging someone's presence is

always important) and show them the discount I'm referring to and ask if it is still available.

2. **PHONE A FRIEND** – The ITV gameshow *Who Wants To Be A Millionaire* taught me a lot about life as well as money/saving. You can't do life alone and you also won't know all the answers yourself. The same can be applied to discounts. It's worth asking your friends, or friends of friends, who maybe work at a particular place, if they could get you a discount. On a number of occasions I have been audacious enough to ask for quite a few things, however I also ensure I ask for things sparingly. Space out your favours, and always offer one in return if you can.

3. **JUST ASK** – A simple thing to do in the moment is just ask. Simple. The best person to approach is always going to be the person in charge. However, if they are not available, speak to whoever is available with politeness and ask if there is a better price than the one you can currently see.

4. **DO YOUR RESEARCH** – A little research into price comparisons can also save you from paying full price. My current phone bill, for example, is a mere £12. I get 15 GB of data, unlimited texts and

unlimited calls. Every year without fail I negotiate my phone bill to a lower amount and let them know what their competitors are offering. Back up what you're saying with a URL link or a code, though, otherwise you could be making it up! Also, when it's time to upgrade, if you choose not to get a new handset, ask for free extras instead. I recently got Disney+ for free for 6 months (and, yup, you guessed it, I watched *Black Is King*). Negotiate as often as you can, as this skill is needed in all areas of your life and the more you practise, the better. It's also important to note that not all great offers are found online. Pick up the phone and call some companies once in a while.

LIFESTYLE HACKS

1. **MAKE A PACKED LUNCH** – There's a popular saying among the black diaspora: 'There's rice at home', meaning it is cheaper to eat what's in your house than what's in the store. As much as I love Pret A Manger, my bank balance isn't so inexhaustible as to make it an a day purchase. And yet there was a time when I used to spend £15 a day on food. One day, I calculated that was £300 a month and £3,600 a year. If I put that £3,600 in a

Lifetime ISA, I'd get £900 as a bonus from the government. Think long term. Those meals aren't always worth it. So, three to four times a week when I work in an office, I bring in food from home. I've spoken on countless panels where people say, 'I don't have the time.' Believe me, if you have time for Netflix shows or the latest series on iPlayer, you've got time to prepare a packed lunch for the week. Go to the shops on a free day and then make sandwiches in bulk for the week, or something else nutritious and filling. What you make is up to you – there is endless inspiration online, just make sure that you get it done.

2. **AVOID RENTING IN CENTRAL CITIES** – If you live at home with parents or guardians, thank your lucky stars. Use that time to act as if you do pay rent and put some extra money away towards your future. If you don't live at home, then it is in your best interests to avoid the inner circle of any other major city. According to *Homes & Property*, rents are rising by up to 21% and the cheapest London borough to live in is Bexley.*

---

* www.homesandproperty.co.uk/property-news/renting/top-10-cheapest-areas-to-rent-in-london-new-report-reveals-bexley-borough-offers-the-most-affordable-a100691.html

Something to factor in to your decision on where to live is that remote working is the future. So even if your job is based in a major city, it doesn't mean you have to live close to your workplace if you are only required to go in a few times a month.

3. **TAKE CHEAPER TRANSPORT** – Between the train, tram, tube, bus, taxi and cycling, there are so many ways to get to your destination. However, some means of transport cost more than others, so it's important to assess which journey is the least costly in conjunction with the time you have available to get to your endpoint. For example, consider getting the bus, and see if you can build in the time regularly. You may well be able to get a seat and a chance to read a book or answer some emails. In future, always consider the most cost-effective option and plan ahead. Speed often equates to cost, but a slower journey may actually be more pleasant as well as costing you significantly less. As with packing a lunch, being organised pays off.

4. **MAKE A LIST** – I find you are far more likely to spend less money in a store when you have a good idea of what you want beforehand. It's

always worth making a list, not just for food but for fashion items too. Having clarity regarding your wants and needs can help prevent impulse purchasing.

5. **UTILISE 'HAPPY HOUR'** – If you are planning on meeting up with a few friends, it's well worth going out when the atmosphere is lively and the drinks are half price. Just as importantly, some food items may be discounted at this time too, so double check when Happy Hour is at bars near you, so that you and your friends can have a great time on a friendly budget.

LEARN TO NEGOTIATE

No one is going to see your value if you don't see it first. Saving isn't always cutting back; it's also asking for more, in the professional sphere and elsewhere. The first time I was offered money to talk about money, after years of working for free trying to prove my value, I was so happy. When you're starting out, you often embrace each new opportunity with open arms and do the work for free, but, sooner or later, and with a lot of hard work and a touch of luck, everything starts to align, and you realise you need to get paid your worth in cash rather than just exposure.

1. **ASK FOR A RAISE** – The first step in asking for a raise is knowing who to approach. Once you know, ask for a meeting regarding your performance at the company. If there is someone you can confide in at work, it's often worth telling them your plans and seeing if they have any tips. When the meeting comes, demonstrate all the reasons why you deserve a raise. It could be your attendance, punctuality, hitting key performance indicators and your attention to detail. These are just some examples to start with, but you know what you do well, so make sure you present that to the right party.

2. **KNOW YOUR FEE** – If you work freelance, before a company asks you to work with them (the key words being 'work with' as opposed to 'work for'), make sure you have a minimum and maximum number in your head. It's always good to have a range and be willing to negotiate. Ask what the company's budget is, and, if applicable, how your work will be used and how long it will be used for. Think about ownership and longevity. How do you want your name to be associated with a particular company?

Learn to be your own representation if you don't yet have any. Here are some great initial steps when approached:

1. Start by being appreciative that you've been considered.

2. Feel free to let them know your current commitments.

3. Ask if there is a budget, a brief, a deadline and payment terms (7 days, 14 days, for example) and if this is based on completion or is an advance payment worth considering, with the balance on delivery.

4. Find out if they offer equal payment to all involved. This means that everyone who is involved is paid the same amount.

5. Enquire if there is a deadline regarding your response, so that you can ensure you get back to them in good time.

6. Google the company, check all their social media, find out about their ethics and ask yourself, does it align with your values?

7. Make a decision and get back to them in a timely manner.

MEET IN THE MIDDLE

My 'aunty' (at least in my head), Michelle Obama, famously said, 'When they go low, we go high.' This saying of hers became well known in 2016 when the First Lady spoke about how to respond when facing challenges.

I agree wholeheartedly with the sentiment, but sometimes I also say, 'Let's meet somewhere in the middle.' Some companies come to me with a low budget and, when I ask for more, they have more excuses than my younger self used to when I didn't want to go to school because I'd fallen out with a friend. At one point I complained to my manager, 'I'm tired of explaining my value to companies.' I was so frustrated that, after five years of freelancing, I was still having to explain what I bring to the table. It is one of the many reasons why I have always kept a salaried job, in addition to my freelance work (and, writing this in 2020, I am very glad I have always done both, because a singular stream of income is not enough).

Every company has different financial priorities, but it's important you don't play your value down as a result of assuming they do not have the budget. At times, with pricing, I've gone extremely high and then realised the company didn't have the money. I sometimes then go back and ask what they do have. And if I get more than I am expecting and I don't need the money, I give it to a cause that's important to me, such as therapy for black people and extracurricular activities for kids.

DON'T RESPOND TO EVERYTHING

Generally speaking, there isn't enough time to respond to everyone in life. Some people will even be super shady to you just so they can get your attention, which is called 'negging'. This can happen in your day job too. If certain duties don't fit into your job description, it's okay to say so. You can point out what your duties are in a polite and professional manner. I used to work for a company till 11 p.m. sometimes. I'll never do that again, because when the pandemic hit they had no problem telling me where to go, however much overtime I'd put in. A company will always look after the company first. Negotiate for what you want but don't confuse it with your true value.

As a woman, all the above can feel even more difficult, but while I don't encourage everyone to take on this burden, I often think about how me not asking for more affects the next woman in question. Do it for you, but also for the next person.

BE REAL WITH YOURSELF

I can't emphasise enough that you need to care about everything you save and spend on down to the last penny. But it's not always that easy. There have been so many times when I've wanted to buy something, just because. Eventually, when I do catch myself and remember that this is the wrong mentality and that keeping to good habits will give me far more satisfaction in the long run.

CHAPTER 4

DEBT

EVERYONE HAS DEBT

Here's the thing: until you deal with your debt, budgeting and saving will feel like a harsh reality. Your debt won't go away on its own and you can't escape it by paying the minimum or ignoring it completely. When you're in debt, it can sometimes feel as if every purchase you make is the wrong decision, but you still have to continue to live, irrespective of your current circumstances. You can't just opt out of spending altogether.

Debt can feel like such a weight holding you down, but it shouldn't. The good news is that you're not alone. So many people are in debt, and I mean that in a good way. Don't let debt take control of *you*. Instead, take control of *it*.

DEBT AND CREDIT EXPLAINED

Debt and credit are quite similar, in some ways. When you have debt, it means that you owe someone or an entity money. Credit is something that is given to you. Whenever you choose to use a credit card, it means that you have entered into an agreement that you will pay back a particular sum, or the entire balance, at a later date, and most companies tend to charge interest in exchange for allowing you to use that line of credit. This arrangement can be great if you maybe need more time to pay for certain purchases. A holiday comes to mind. It is not always that you can't pay for the holiday in one go, but maybe you need to think about all the other costs you currently have and spread your outgoings over time? On the basis that you have good discipline, the best thing to do would be to start making your holiday payments with a credit card. That way you get the benefit of purchase protection, you can pay in instalments, and, as long as you pay your balance back on time, it can also boost your credit score.

TYPES OF DEBT

When people think about debt, they generally mean using their credit card or hitting their overdraft, but think about store cards too. There are many forms of debt and it can be quite confusing. Here is a quick breakdown of the different types of debt that you should know about.

1. **BUSINESS DEBT** – For those who have a registered company, this is anything the company owes to another company. This could

take the form of secured or unsecured loans. The difference between the two is that the former is secured against any assets you have, such as your home.

2. **CONSUMER CREDIT** – This is personal debt you use to pay for goods and services. An example would be using a credit card.

3. **CONTRACT DEBT** – Common examples are mortgages, bonds, and loans. A mortgage is a legal way by which a bank or building society lends money at interest in exchange for taking title of the debtor's property. A bond, meanwhile, is what's called a fixed income instrument that represents a loan made by an investor to a borrower (typically corporate or governmental). Lastly, a loan is a sum of money expected to be paid back with interest.

4. **COURT DEBT AND FINES** – Court debt is no joke, and is known as a County Court Judgement (CCJ). If you decide to ignore creditors, they can pass it on to a debt collection agency and it can continue to escalate from there. This escalation can result in bailiffs at your door or a CCJ being put on your record.

Fines are also something that can escalate. Anyone who drives knows the gut-wrenching pain of finding a yellow ticket on their car. Don't ignore these or think you're above the law. Some people risk it, but this country has no mercy. I assure you that no one is exempt from paying up, so make sure you pay all forms of fine (after you've appealed, where appropriate, of course).

5. **DEBTS TO OTHERS** – This is what you owe your family and/or friends. Keep your relationships in good standing by not letting money get in the way. Be as honest about your situation as possible. Also, don't avoid the people who have loaned you money if you can't make a payment on time, as this can feel really hurtful when someone has trusted you with their money. Honour your relationship with honesty, even if it's difficult.

6. **GOVERNMENT DEBT** – This is also known as public debt. This is the current debt the government owes to creditors within the country as well as internationally.

7. **HOUSEHOLD DEBT** – The calculation of household debt is based on the amount of debt that

everyone who currently lives at a particular address has collectively, and is usually thought about in the form of your family.

8. **JOINT DEBTS** – This is any debt that you have jointly with your spouse. It's really important that we think about who we are joining with not just on an emotional level but also on a financial one, as, when you're married, their debts become your debts and vice versa.

9. **PAYDAY LOAN DEBT** – Payday loans tend to incur a significant amount of interest. Where possible, avoid them at all costs. A payday loan is a win for the company lending you the money, essentially, and it can leave you with a big hole in your pocket that wasn't worth it even in the short term, because you end up paying substantially more in the long run.

10. **STUDENT LOAN DEBT** – Student loan debt is anything that goes towards your further education. This includes tuition fees, maintenance loans and postgraduate lines of credit. What's great is that there is no need for you to pay back any grants or loans until you reach a certain threshold of earnings.

GOOD DEBT VS BAD DEBT

The concept of debt can be a confusing one. So, let's clear up some debt mysteries.

Good debt is when you make an investment in your future that will reap benefits long term. This can also be seen as a future return on investment. What must be remembered is that good debt still requires strategy and tenacity. Some examples of good debt are a student loan, a mortgage, and investing in your own business.

1. **A STUDENT LOAN** – Femi goes to university from 2015–2018 and comes out with £40k of debt. By 2020, Femi is earning £40k per year, far more than if he had no qualifications. By 2025, Femi is earning £120k. His education has made him more money than his education cost.

2. **A MORTGAGE** – Sadiq bought a house in Essex for £250k in 2010 in the hope that the value of the property would appreciate over time. He has been renting it out for the last ten years. In 2020, the world faces a recession and Sadiq needs to liquidate some of his assets to keep financially afloat. Sadiq sells his Essex home for £320k. In

ten years, Sadiq has made an additional £70k as the price of the house has gone up.

Bad debts, meanwhile, are those that lower your net worth and your overall wealth. These are debts that cost you more over time, such as a car that you can't afford, going on a holiday outside of your budget, and borrowing or using your credit card in an unsustainable way. This is not shade, this is real life.

GETTING IT DOWN

Here's how to get started. Get a piece of paper or open up a new spreadsheet and draw five columns. Head those columns with the following:

1. Debt Type – e.g. Loan, Overdraft, Personal.

2. Company/Person – Who are you in debt to?

3. Purpose of Debt – Why are you in this situation? (It can be quite surprising when you're confronted with the why behind your debt.)

4. Amount Owed.

5. APR – if any.

I find we rarely appreciate how much we are paying particular companies until we tally it up. One of my clients felt so disgusted after she saw the full cost of her debts, including APR, and vowed on the spot never to pay that much again. A lot of these companies prey on financial illiteracy, but now you have this book, you're going to do better.

Remember, when our finances feel out of our control, always return to the drawing board. We all fall down, but we can't stay there. Get up every single day and know that this too shall pass.

GETTING OUT OF IT

Once you've tallied everything, it's time to figure out how you're going to get out of this situation.

1. Number each debt from the most important to the least.

2. Figure out how much a particular debt is costing you in total, how much you have to pay and what you need to contribute regularly to clear it.

3. Choose a debt reduction strategy (see below) and apply it.

The three main types of debt reduction strategy are as follows and can be adapted to suit you:

DEBT REDUCTION STRATEGY #1

HIGHEST INTEREST RATE FIRST

The harsh reality is that the debt with the highest APR is likely to be costing you the most money, no matter what the balance is. So, for example, if you have a credit card debt that you're paying 39% APR on each month, that should be your focus. The theory behind this method is that you make this debt a priority and put the rest on a backburner (while still keeping up minimum payments).

DEBT REDUCTION STRATEGY #2

DEBT SNOWBALL

In this method, the debt with the smallest balance is paid off first and minimum payments are made on larger debts. The next step is to pay off the next smallest debt. It may sound counterintuitive, but the advantage of this is psychological, as you may feel that wiping out one debt completely gives you the momentum needed to keep going. An 'easy win' gives you the motivation to continue.

DEBT REDUCTION STRATEGY #3

DEBT CONSOLIDATION

This method depends on your eligibility to take out another form of credit, but it may well cost you less to have one loan than three different forms of credit with varying APRs.

SPEAK TO SOMEONE

Something you might be dreading is calling the companies you owe money to, but they aren't there to judge you, they are there to help you. Don't avoid the situation, because it can really affect your credit score if you stick your head in the sand. Let them know your current situation and what you can afford to pay. Some of them may be lenient and some may not be. As I said earlier, it always pays to negotiate. There is no point paying more than you can manage. All it will do is give you anxiety. If the person on the phone isn't particularly understanding of your situation, ask to speak to someone higher up. You are well within your rights to do so. Most banks, building societies and other lenders train their staff to deal with these sorts of conversations, and I can guarantee they will have heard far worse than your particular case.

DEALING WITH DENIAL

You may have heard of the Kübler-Ross model, which measures/outlines the five stages of grief. I would argue that there are also five stages of debt.

STAGE ONE: DENIAL

Financial setbacks almost always start innocently. You can so easily fall behind on a bill or forget that parking fine, or you may be going through life-changing circumstances that have knocked you off course. You begin to see the reality of your situation can be tough, and you may choose to believe it is not the case, as it feels easier. However, the longer you do that, the more debt you put yourself into.

STAGE TWO: FACING THE REALITY

Once you've overcome denial and accepted your financial situation, it's time to put pen to paper and get into the intricacies of what you need to pay off, how urgent each debt is and when you think you can pay it back. Doing this may require some quiet time, it may require a cup of coffee or even a glass of wine. Nonetheless, set the mood and begin to get into the details.

STAGE THREE: OVERWHELMED

Once you do start putting pen to paper, however, it is easy to feel overwhelmed as you begin to add up the numbers. Remember: you are not on this journey alone. Some companies are even willing to help you for free if you feel you cannot handle the situation by yourself. However, you'll find you also have a ready-made support system if you're prepared to reach out. It is okay to let someone know how you're feeling about your financial situation. We share so many aspects of our lives, so we should be able to share our money situation as well. While you may be experiencing a range of emotions, avoid the temptation to beat yourself up. For the past is just that: it's already gone and now it's time to look at today and work towards your debt-free goal.

STAGE FOUR: ENDURANCE

We all know the beginning of anything can be a bit tedious. However, once you get into the rhythm of paying off your debt and start building momentum, you will gradually realise that you are making progress and getting ever closer to the finish line, which can be exhilarating but also takes endurance and tenacity. It is important that you persevere, consider how far you've come, and congratulate yourself, instead of fixating on how far you've got to go. Most importantly, try not to obsess about the amount of time it's taking you to pay off the debt. And beware of comparing yourself to others, because some people's debts take them three months to pay off, some take three years to pay off, and some even longer. And what about all those people who have mortgages, which means they may be paying off a house loan for thirty years? Paying off your debts is not a competition between you and the future you. Paying off your debts is about getting closer to the best version of your financial life.

STAGE FIVE: FREEDOM

Paying off all your debts can be one of the best feelings in the world and, when you get to that point, you should celebrate, because it can be an emotional experience. For all the sacrifices you've had to make, the moment you know you are debt-free is the moment you can breathe a little better and look forward to saving, spending more responsibly and looking ahead to the future. Whether that future is a holiday house or further education or any other dream, the world is your oyster.

YOUR MENTAL HEALTH AND DEBT

As someone who has been in debt and had major anxiety as a result of it, I cannot tell you how pointless the time I lost to those demons was. Always remember – every situation is temporary. Don't amplify your situation with needless overthinking. As a result of trying to be a solo entrepreneur in 2019, I got into some debt. It felt super embarrassing to be the person who champions finances, yet there I was sitting with debt I couldn't control. I couldn't buy clothes, I couldn't really go on holiday, and it felt very hard explaining my situation to my loved ones. I didn't want their help, though, because I thought it was an important lesson for me to learn. And it was.

One of the best things you can do for your mental health when it comes to your finances is open up and tell the truth to those who won't judge you for it. The reality is life is hard and it's always throwing you curveballs. Whatever you're going through financially doesn't make you a loser in *any* capacity. We should never be defined by how much money we have. Capitalism has warped us on what is truly important. Some of the best lessons I have learned have come out of financial hardship, as it forced me to become resourceful and take pleasure in the things that money couldn't buy. These have now become some of my favourite things in life. Going for a walk is free. Having more time to think about what you really want from life during tough times can also be free. However you can, try and find a silver lining to your situation. It won't be bad for ever, but don't add to the stresses of life by thinking too intensely beyond the day in front of you.

So, to recap, here are a few steps you can take to get in front of your debt:

1. Call those you owe money to and set up a payment plan that works for you.

2. Note all your standing orders, direct debits and credit card payments on your phone calendar, and create a regular reminder.

3. Don't be afraid to ask for help, and know where to find it. There are some helpful resources on page 121.

CHAPTER 5

CREDIT

USE CREDIT, DON'T LET CREDIT USE YOU

Many financial gurus say credit cards are the devil, and billionaire philanthropist and investor Warren Buffett doesn't see the point in using them. With that being said, some people are not in the position of privilege to be able to do without a credit card and in some situations they can actually be beneficial.

PROS

1. **PURCHASE PROTECTION** – This means that, in the event anything goes wrong with what you've purchased, you are protected by the Consumer Credit Act, under section 75, for any item that is £100 and over. No debit card will give you this.

   Once, I got stranded in Nigeria and had to book a new flight back to London using my own money. If I had booked that flight on my credit card, my credit card company would have been able to assist me in getting my money back if the airline in question was of no help. So, any time I make major purchases, I tend to make them on my credit card.

2. **IMPROVE YOUR CREDIT SCORE** – Having a credit card can actually improve your credit score, believe it or not. Some people say that there is no need to have one and it's, of course, completely within your right to choose not to, however I know people who have not been able to buy a house because the lender has not been able to see enough history of them demonstrating being able to pay back credit. If there is no history of how you handle repayments, then anyone lending money to you may not be sure of your ability to pay it back.

CONS

1. **SELF-DISCIPLINE** – You have to have a fantastic level of discipline if you are planning to use a credit card or take on any form of debt. Treating yourself on your credit card can become a dangerous game, especially if you are not Cher from *Clueless*, who had a rich father And even if you do have a rich father willing to bail you out, think about the repercussions of spending on a credit card without thinking. Someone has to pay it back and it can be a painful process. If you lack discipline with your

finances, I would say it's best that you stay clear of credit cards.

2. **MISSED PAYMENTS/LATE FEES** – Missing payments can affect your credit score significantly. What I've actually found that missing a payment isn't always to do with not having money. Some people miss payments because they are busy, which is why you always have to stay on top of your financial admin. Once the late fee shows up on your credit card statement, it can flag alerts to other lenders that you are not taking care of your credit.

TIP

Pay off more than the bare minimum.
If you choose to pay the lowest amount back, you'll be paying off your credit card forever. The credit card company will enjoy this, because they are taking money from you through interest and will get far more in the long run. The quicker you make it a priority to pay off your credit card, the freer you will feel.

FINDING A CREDIT CARD THAT SUITS YOU

I used to get so many letters from companies telling me that I was eligible for their credit card back in the day, even though I hadn't applied for any of them. Being accepted in any format can make you feel proud and happy to be 'chosen', but you must remember that every time somebody offers you something, you should ask yourself what they are getting out of it. These companies are not your friends – they are businesses. And don't forget your money is *your* business.

One of my earliest mistakes was going with a credit card company just because it was who I banked with. I wasn't happy with my APR and I didn't even know what my benefits were. There are so many options out there – 0% balance transfer credit cards, 0% to purchase credit cards, balance transfer and purchase credit cards, credit-building credit cards, cashback credit cards, reward credit cards and money transfer credit cards.

1. **0% BALANCE TRANSFER CREDIT CARD** – Can help you pay off your outstanding credit card debt by moving the balance from one card (or multiple

cards) where you might be paying high rates of interest, to a new one at a 0% interest rate for a set period of time.

2. **PURCHASE CREDIT CARD** – Designed for shopping, it lets you make purchases and spread the cost over a period of time.

3. **CREDIT-BUILDING CREDIT CARD** – Good for people with no credit or bad credit who want to improve their credit score.

4. **REWARD CREDIT CARD** – Can offer you perks, such as free flights and money off your supermarket shop.

5. **MONEY TRANSFER CREDIT CARD** – Pays cash straight into your bank account.

There are plenty of websites, such as Compare the Market and Moneysupermarket.com, which can help you decide which card could suit your needs best. Remember, don't just go for the first good deal you see. If there is one good deal, it's likely there are a dozen others. Remember *your* money is *your* business, so make sure you are getting the best deal.

Also, be aware that a lot of companies use psychological marketing tricks to get you to buy products that you don't need. This includes credit cards that you didn't plan to take out or loans that you do not need. Think of any credit card advert that appears on television – they usually start with a very bright and appealing voice that catches your attention and entices you in. Then, when it comes to the terms and conditions, all of a sudden, the voice speeds up. This is not an accident. Know exactly what you're getting into with any company you choose to partner with. So often we forget that everything is a partnership in some form, including our money. We can't and we shouldn't take that for granted.

READ THE SMALL PRINT

Here's an example of how important it is to read the small print:

> Farrukh moved from Pakistan to London. In London, everybody is keeping up with somebody else.
> In Pakistan, Farrukh never heard much about credit, but, in the UK, it is widely available. Farrukh wants a job in the city and sees men wearing suits from

T. M. Lewin that cost £400. Farrukh can only afford one suit at the moment but he wants a job quickly and feels as if one is not enough. A company we'll call Instant Gratification tells him he is eligible for a credit card today that will give him a £2,000 limit. Farrukh doesn't think twice, he gets the card and he buys five suits that very day. Farrukh can only contribute a maximum of £200 per month to his credit card as he has other financial responsibilities.

Farrukh didn't read the small print. The APR is 39%. This works out at a monthly minimum payment of £198.32 based on him reaching his limit. Total cost of credit: £379.84 based on an APR of 39% That's a total of: £2,379.84.

It is important to note that a credit card or any other form of lending is not in itself good or bad; it is about how you utilise it. Only Farrukh will know if the suits were worth it. The same goes for luxury goods and everything else the human heart desires.

THE CREDIT SCORE GAME

The only time 999, the number you dial in an emergency in the UK, is used in a purely positive way is when you look at your credit score. This is considered an excellent score, depending on the lender.

When it comes to your credit score – the number that lenders refer to that determines the likelihood of you being able to take out credit, and what risk you pose and therefore rate of interest you will need to pay – there are three main credit reference agencies in the UK: Experian, Equifax and TransUnion.

Credit reference agencies are independent organisations that hold data, such as when you apply for credit, any accounts that you have and your attitude towards your finances. This information helps companies decide whether or not they would like to lend particular amounts to customers. In the UK, credit scores tend to range from 0 to 999. A credit score that is considered fair will be anything from 721 to 880, good is considered 881 to 960, and excellent is 960 to 999.

The reason I called this section the 'credit score game' is because I find credit scores to be quite fickle. One minute your score may be excellent, but if you don't use your credit card for a period of time, your score can also drop. As your balances differ over time, your score fluctuates from month to month. If you are looking to improve your credit score, here are some great tips to get you started:

1. **USE YOUR CREDIT WISELY** – Do you have a credit account that you don't use? If you're noticing that your credit score is quite stagnant, it may be because you are not utilising the credit that you have. Using your credit card but ensuring you pay it off in full each month can improve matters.

2. **LOOK AT YOUR PAST** – Certain financial blunders can affect your credit card and score for up to six or seven years. It is worth disputing your defaults or late payments, if you have any in your financial history. Getting those removed from your credit report could boost your score.

3. **ERRORS ON YOUR REPORT** – It's important to check your credit report regularly. Does anything look out of the ordinary? If so, dispute it. Another important thing to note is that if you have a very similar name to someone in your family or you have the same date of birth as someone in your family, the credit companies could be confusing the two of you. You won't know it's a problem until you check your report, so make sure that you do.

4. **YOUR CREDIT UTILISATION IS TOO HIGH** – A credit utilisation ratio is the total credit you've used or owe divided by your total credit limit across all your accounts. This ratio is seen as a good indicator of how you are looking after your money and is usually written as a percentage.

   For example, Ore has a £6,000 total limit across his credit accounts. If he uses £3,000 then his credit utilisation is 50%. It is a generally accepted rule of thumb that it's best to be under 30% of your credit utilisation at any time. Studies show that those with high credit scores only use about 1–10% of their limit.

To stay on top of your credit utilisation, try setting up balance alerts so you know what to do if you're about to hit a particular number.

YOUR CREDIT REPORT (AND HOW IT DIFFERS FROM A CREDIT SCORE)

Think of a credit report as the report card your parents or guardians were given when you were in school. Your credit report shows how you've behaved with your finances over the last six years. Absolutely everything is included in this report, from your mortgage to any overdraft or loans you've had, any phone contracts or utilities you've held in your name. You can go to one of the credit reference agencies mentioned earlier to get hold of this report. It's worth doing. You can also get credit reports for free with companies like Credit Karma, however, with some other companies it's likely that you'll have to pay for this information.

The youngest age at which you are eligible for credit is eighteen, so ensure this is reflected on your credit report. Anything that looks out of order should be queried. Companies like Experian offer a free trial, where you can see your credit history in the form of a basic statutory report.

TIP

Remember to cancel your free trial before the end date, otherwise it could cost you money.

How often you choose to check your credit report is up to you. It's worth having a look at it when you change address or when you apply for credit, and especially if you're worried about any form of identity theft. Some people check their credit report every month and some not at all. I know it's not the most exciting thing to do, but it's worth knowing where you stand when it comes to your credit report and your credit score.

HOW DEBT AFFECTS YOUR CREDIT

There are times when one form of credit just isn't enough and you may need to make some calls and apply for a different type of credit. While this may seem daunting, it's not always a bad thing. Taking out different types of credit can have advantages and disadvantages. The most common type is a loan.

PROS OF TAKING OUT A LOAN:

1. You can pay back what you owe over a period of time that suits your situation. For example, you can take out a loan for £10,000 and choose to pay that back in one year or even ten years. The duration you choose is completely up to you. However, it's important to note that you may pay more on the loan if you choose to borrow for a longer time.

2. On the basis that you stick within the terms and conditions of the type of credit you chose to take out, your credit score can increase because you have shown that you are able to keep up with your payments. This makes a great case for you if you decide that later on you would like to take out a mortgage.

CONS OF TAKING OUT A LOAN:

1. You don't want to get trapped into a cycle of being in debt. There is no point taking out a loan and forgetting how much it's going to cost you to pay it back. A common phrase I hear in my line of work is 'I thought I'd finished paying it off.' Make sure you have all the information and the debt repayment plan in place.

2. Depending on your credit score, the interest rates on some loans may be higher.

3. Be careful of loan sharks. A 'loan shark' is defined as a person or an entity that loans money at extremely high interest rates, and often uses threats of violence to collect debts. Companies that offer you money with a quick turnaround are something to be wary of. Make sure the company

you're looking at has a good reputation. All it takes is a few moments on Google to read the reviews on websites such as Trustpilot. I always tend to notice that the worst loans with ridiculous APRs are advertised on minor commercial channels. In my opinion, these companies prey on those that they know don't have the discipline to say no, even if it is a bad deal.

YOUR OVERDRAFT

An overdraft is what your bank allows you to borrow from your current account. You can often set your own overdraft limit and, once again, how much you can get depends on how good your credit is. The great thing about overdrafts is the flexibility; usually, you are only charged a percentage based on how much of the overdraft you use. The main downfall is the fact that an overdraft can't be used if you'd like to borrow a large amount, and, on top of that, the rate of interest tends to be higher than for loans.

A key tip is to keep well within the limit of your overdraft. Do *not* go over your limit, because your bank notices everything. There was a time when I was going over my limit by about a pound or two a month, which seemed like nothing. Then, one day, I decided I wanted to increase my overdraft limit. When I called the bank, they said I couldn't get an increase as a result of how I was treating my current overdraft.

ARRANGED AND UNARRANGED OVERDRAFTS

Arranged overdrafts and unarranged overdrafts – it's as simple as it sounds. An arranged overdraft is one you agree with the bank, and an unarranged overdraft is when you didn't agree to it beforehand and you have chosen to go overdrawn. Any overdraft you have appears on your credit report as a debt, however, and if you don't use your overdraft it shows a zero balance.

Overdrafts don't have a big impact on your credit score (unless you go over into an unarranged overdraft), but make sure you keep up to date with what you owe and don't get comfortable being in the red. Many students get offered 0% on their overdraft and the real surprise comes when they graduate and have to pay it back. There is no such thing as free money, so make sure that you are using that 0% interest to the best of your ability while you have it.

DON'T LET OTHERS USE YOUR CREDIT

So many clients have come to me with horror stories of how family members or friends have asked them to take out different forms of credit in their name. This could be a gas bill, a phone bill, or even payment for a new boiler. This is a form of manipulation, and I hate it.

Only one person has to live with their credit score, and that's you. To put the onus on someone else to take care of your life is not living at all. As often as possible, shield yourself from people who ask you to put your name to things that can impact you financially. I see this most often with people who don't have good relationships with their family. Call me insensitive, but your family feuds are not you and your credit's business. Don't feel pressured into saying yes. Saying yes is a long-term commitment, and you have no idea how that person's character and your relationship with them may change over time. If someone decides that they want to stop talking to you or they want to stop paying a bill, they may have less of a concern for how that affects you because their name is not on it.

CHAPTER 6

INVEST

INVEST IN YOU FIRST

So often, when we get paid, the first person we forget to pay is ourselves. Let this book be a continuous reminder to you that *you* are worth putting first. Without you, there are no bills, there are no clothes, there are no fun times with the people you love. Pay yourself first and I don't mean just in savings.

There are dreams, visions and ventures that you may have in your mind that you have kept sealed, as if in a jar. Every time you get paid, lift the lid of the jar and invest in the dreams that you truly believe in. This may sound like something from a corny after-school special, but our time is limited, as Steve Jobs once said, and we shouldn't waste it living a life we don't want to. Of course, nothing happens overnight, but a little step every day goes a long way, often more than we can sometimes imagine. I don't always think about the whole journey, as when I do it gives me mental fatigue, but just take one step at a time. Your finances can be the key to achieving your goals.

RETURN ON INVESTMENT

In life, there will always be people who expect a return on their investment, on the time they feel they put in to you, even if you didn't ask them to. Financial boundaries are not spoken about enough, often because of the constant guilt that some of us are made to feel by those who are close to us. While it is a beautiful sentiment to help the ones you love, including your immediate family, you are under no obligation to pay them back for everything they did for you.

Emotional guilt as well as financial guilt often has people staying in relationships, environments and spaces that don't serve them, all because someone, or a group of people, uses manipulation as a way to keep them hostage.

Here are ways to set financial boundaries between you and your loved ones.

1. **SET YOUR OWN RULES** – What usually starts as a one-off amount can soon become a regular occurrence. When you are a natural giver, people will come to you. It is both a blessing and a curse. People should be allowed to give freely as and when they feel the urge to do so. It should not be an expectation. Put aside an amount within your budget that you are okay with giving away each month to family. Under

no circumstances should you put yourself last and them first. It doesn't matter what the occasion or the emergency is. Make sure that there is always enough for you to live on before you give money to other people.

2. **SET TERMS AND CONDITIONS** – This might seem overly formal, but it is important that you and who you're lending the money to are on the same page. You don't want to be in a situation where you expected money on the 15th of the month and the lender thinks it's due on the 30th, or, worse yet, never. I have been in situations where I have loaned people money and then heard their awkward laugh when I bring it up. Money is not a funny topic, especially when you could potentially lose it.

Once you've made it clear how much you can lend, ask them when they plan to pay it back and if there is anything that you need to know that may hinder this happening. Remember that when someone really needs money, they are more likely to react out of a form of desperation. However, time and time again I've heard stories of people becoming nonchalant when it comes to paying it back. This leads me on to my next point.

3. **COMMUNICATION IS A MUST** – I don't believe that you should chase anyone for anything. You shouldn't have to hunt someone down to get your money back. However, when the day comes when that person has to pay you back, kindly and politely message them, if you haven't heard from them already. If that fails, give them a call. If for any reason that person is not responding to any form of communication, I send them something like this as a last resort.

'Hey, I hope you're well and everyone is blessed. I don't know what's going on, but we agreed that today would be the date you paid me back. If circumstances have changed, just let me know, but I'd prefer if our relationship doesn't alter because of money.'

At this point, I leave it up to the universe to sort it out. I do not lend anything I am afraid of losing, and I am more afraid of losing the relationship. However, we don't have control over everything and that includes how people choose to react to situations surrounding money.

4. **JUST SAY NO** – It may seem a bit harsh, but we are not responsible for other people's livelihoods unless we have chosen legally for it to be so. Yes, we can all fall on hard times, and this is exactly where you should use your discernment to decide if you want to help someone. Nevertheless, don't let anyone bully you into giving what you don't have to spare. The emphasis here is on *spare*. Just because you have a tenner it doesn't mean that you should give that tenner away to others. Give when you can and when it makes financial sense to you. Don't let anybody else count your pockets but you. If you ever fall on hard times yourself, you never want to look back at the person you gave money to with regret and resentment. Don't let manipulation win. It is the easiest trick in the book to strong arm those who are vulnerable, so be wary of triggers. If you feel as if someone is gaslighting you to get under your skin or into your bank account, speak to someone else you trust for clarification. At times, the conversations we have with ourselves are not enough for us to see we are being taken advantage of, so be sure to have the conversation with someone else too.

INVESTING FOR BEGINNERS

Before you start investing, there are some terms you'll need to familiarise yourself with.

1. **SECURITY** – A security is a financial instrument. It represents ownership of different types of securities, such as debt securities, equity securities and derivatives. An example of a debt security is a bond. An example of an equity security is a stock, and an example of a derivative is an option.

2. **BOND** – A bond is when you loan money to the government or banks and they use the money to finance other projects. When you listen to or read the news about what the government is doing, they may be using bonds to fund their activities. You are paid interest on the bond, and you receive your money back at the end of the agreed period. A bond issued by the UK government is called a gilt.

3. **STOCKS** – Stocks meet equity, equity meet stocks. Equity and stocks are essentially one and the same. Once you buy stocks in a company it means you own a part of the company. How much you own is up to you and your financial

situation. Stocks are a lot more unpredictable than bonds and are dependent on a variety of factors.

4. **STOCK MARKET** – The stock market is where stocks and bonds are traded, meaning where they are bought and sold. The main stock exchange for the UK is the LSE (London Stock Exchange). The Financial Times Stock Exchange (FTSE) 100 are the most dominant companies listed on the LSE. If you ever hear the term 'Footsie', this is what people are referring to. The S&P 500, meanwhile, charts the performance of 500 large companies in the US. FTSE 100, S&P 500, Dow Jones and NASDAQ are all well known market indexes.

5. **INDEXES** – Indexes tend to measure the performance of many securities with the intention of replicating particular areas of the market.

6. **DIVERSIFICATION** – Diversification means having a variety of investments. This is usually done to reduce the risk of your investments, as if one doesn't work out, the others might. Regardless of the reason behind diversifying,

never put all your investments into one pot. Look at all the businesspeople you admire and you'll notice they have a variety of investments. Where feasible, you should too.

THE RIGHT TIME?

There is no particular age or criteria for starting to invest. The most important thing to know is that your capital – the amount of money you put into particular investments – is at risk. You have to have the guts to invest, because your money can go up as much as it can go down. Nonetheless, there are great advantages to investing, such as:

1. **INHERITANCE** – You can pass on particular investments to your children and grandchildren. When my father passed away, I inherited a sum of money because my grandfather was a wealthy man who had invested in everything from stocks to businesses to property and fixed sum cash deposits.

2. **INCOME STREAMS** – Depending on how much you invest, you won't have to rely on one source of income. Having multiple streams of income has stopped me from panicking every time I'm

worried about the stability of the economy or my current job.

3. **RETURNS** – The returns you can make from investments could be much higher than the current interest rate you are getting on your savings or current account. Say, for example, you have £1,000 to either save or invest and the interest rate being offered on the High Street is 1%. You're not exactly making a lot of money and this is why investments are important.

However, before you think about playing with investment, you should consider two things.

1. **DO YOU HAVE ENOUGH SAVINGS?** – The idea of putting all your money into investments that can fluctuate and having little to no savings left over is like getting on The Detonator at Thorpe Park. It's great at the top, but it's the drop to the bottom that can make you question whether you're going to keep your lunch! What constitutes 'enough savings' can only be determined by you. For some people, it may be twelve months of their salary before they start investing. For others it may be more or even less. You choose what you're comfortable with.

2. **DO YOU HAVE AN EMERGENCY FUND?** – What counts as an emergency is, again, completely up to you. I would suggest you start by having between three and six months of all your expenses set aside in an emergency fund. It's important to note that just because it's an emergency fund doesn't mean that you shouldn't try to find the best interest rate for that sum of money. Some of my clients have come to tell me that they have put their funds in pots such as a Monzo pot. While that's great, I never want to hear that your money is not making money. No matter how small, interest is interest.

RISK AND REWARD

There is a phrase you'll often hear financial people use: 'attitude to risk'. In general, there are three main categories.

1. **RISK AVERSE** – This person is reluctant to take risks and they are more likely to accept far lower returns with risks that they are aware of rather than higher returns with risks they cannot see coming.

2. **RISK NEUTRAL** – This is someone who doesn't have a preference towards risk. They focus on the returns that are expected from the investments.

3. **RISK LOVER** – A risk lover is literally willing to risk it all for the higher return. They are the people who want to go on the scariest rides at Thorpe Park because they like the thrill.

Once you understand your appetite for risk, you also need to factor in what your investment goals are. There is no such thing as a genuine get-rich-quick scheme. Anybody who is promising you that is probably trying to scam you out of your money. Remember that people can fake reports and even pretend to be exclusive to make it look like they are the best people to invest with. Ensure that you do your due diligence as much as possible. Before I interact with any company that I want to invest with I do the following checks:

1. **ASK ABOUT THEM** – It's always good to know who else has put their money behind certain companies because it can make you feel at ease with your decision to go forward. Ask family and friends.

2. **CHECK TRUSTPILOT** – What rating does the company have out of five stars? What do people you don't know think about their products or services? Trustpilot is a great place to go to find out how a company is perceived by the general public.

3. **LOOK AT THEIR SOCIAL MEDIA PRESENCE** – It isn't the be all and end all if they don't have a big social media presence, but it's a good way of seeing how they interact with people. Is the presentation of their services clear?

4. **SEE IF THEY ARE REGULATED BY THE FCA** – This is a big factor. FCA stands for Financial Conduct Authority. Being regulated by the FCA means that the company must remain honest, balanced and effective. The three main aims are to protect consumers, protect financial markets and promote competition in the interests of consumers.

5. **GOOGLE THE CEO, BOARD AND STAFF** – It's always key for me to know what the CEO did before and to get a sense of their moral compass. Do they care about climate change? What is the percentage of people from ethnic

backgrounds sitting on the board? How many of the staff are women? How do they support their staff from a corporate social responsibility standpoint? These things matter to me. Know what matters to you before you put your money into a business.

CHAPTER 7

WELLNESS

SAVE YOUR ENERGY AND TIME

In mid 2020, an article came out about me and, from that moment onwards, my phone didn't stop ringing, my emails didn't stop pinging. I was featured in *Forbes* as one of twenty-five leading black British business people in the UK. This led to an avalanche of meetings with people who wanted to give me money, people who wanted to give me opportunities, and people who generally wanted to get to know me. I felt then and I feel now very privileged to have had such opportunities, but that doesn't take away from the fact that I started to feel serious burnout. This burnout also caused me to spend money in unnecessary ways because I felt I didn't have the time to look after myself properly. This meant cooking less, ordering more and not taking the time to do an audit of what I already had. When your wellbeing takes a hit, your financials can fall with it.

It is a scientific fact that the average human has to make about 35,000 conscious decisions every day.* Decision fatigue can be hard on all levels. Whether you

---

* www.psychologytoday.com/gb/blog/stretching-theory/201809/
  how-many-decisions-do-we-make-each-day

are deciding where you want to live or the next step in your child's future. Even deciding what to wear each day can take up mental space. If you look at Mark Zuckerberg, he wears the same thing every day, and there's something to be said for simplifying your options and reducing the number of decisions you face each and every day. I eventually decided to borrow from that approach.

You can start by deciding what is worth your time and what isn't. This can also be applied to what you spend your money on. This idea that society conditions into us, especially women, that you have to please everyone, has to stop if you want to get to where you truly want to be. No one I know has got to where they need to be by being a 'yes' person 24/7. You don't have to take every call, not if it means that your energy for more important things flags as a result. It is great to talk about money, but if you don't have the energy you need to make the money you want to, it is never going to work.

TAKING CARE OF YOU

I'll be honest – nothing annoys me more than 'no sleep' crew. I pride myself on getting enough sleep to function in the best possible way in order to make better decisions. The result of me not getting enough sleep is me becoming irrational, which results in me becoming a lot more emotional and extremely irritated by almost anything and everyone – not good. For me or my money.

Where possible avoid that version of you that is like getting the iPhone 3 in today's world, full of glitches and running slow – we are not at that level any more. When I am tired, I find I make more mistakes with my money, such as purchasing the same item twice. Before I make any big financial decisions, I wait 24–72 hours to ensure it's what I truly want. Do not make decisions when your clarity isn't at an all-time high.

Now, let's move on to what we eat and drink. Think about what you're putting into your body as often as you can. I know we all have our moments where we want to forget, and we just want that sugar rush or any other form of high, but, long term, it's not going to work. Have a healthy balanced diet, eat your fruit and vegetables and drink two litres of water every day. In fact, at times I drink three litres of water a day. Hydration is important in making good decisions. Fizzy drinks, alcohol and coffee are okay from time to time, but they take away from your natural hydration. Do not substitute these things for water.

A phone detox is also very important. Time away from your phone can do wonders for you. Looking into a screen all day is not only bad for your eyes, it is bad for your mind. Think about what you are consuming on a daily basis and whether it is helping or hindering you. Don't forget the amount of ads that are also being pushed your way through different devices such as television and social media apps. Many people I know don't read the news because they can't take the negativity and I don't blame them. Ever since the pandemic, I haven't been able to stop watching the news as a result of what I do for a living, and I can feel the impact of that decision daily. However, there are times when you have to protect your mind more than anything else. There is a well-known saying which is 'if it costs you your peace of mind, it is too expensive'. Absolutely anything that costs you your peace of mind is not worth it. This doesn't mean that you need to be cut off from the world, but it does mean you need to think about your interactions with people that rub you up the wrong way. For example, I have a friend who no matter what day or time it is cannot stop talking about the stock market. Our conversations tend to last a maximum of 10 to 15 minutes, and during that time I'll keep telling them that I don't want to talk about it, that I am a human *being*, I am not a human *doing*. I am more than what I do for a living. We all are. Making money is fantastic and the hope is to use some of that to leave a legacy, but who we are and how we treat people must come before the material things of this world.

You have to remember that you are not a machine. It is okay to rest; it is okay to take time off without there being a reason to do so. If this pandemic has taught us anything, it is that work is not as important as we make it out to be. We tell ourselves that we are doing it for the people we love, but if we don't know how to be present with those very same people we love because we are so worried about work, then work itself is a waste of time. Do you love your work, love yourself and love your people? There is no higher feeling than that. We are all as rich as we feel within ourselves, so make sure as often as possible that you are looking after yourself and your loved ones. It is an investment you will never regret.

CONCLUSION

ALWAYS BET ON YOURSELF

If someone told me five years ago that I'd be publishing a book, I don't know if I would have believed them. A lot of that has to do with how confident I have been in myself and my abilities. While I've always been audacious, I still get nervous. I still question whether or not I can really do something, and it takes a lot of pep talks with myself and my loved ones for me to keep going.

Sure, there are times when I want to pack up everything and disappear into the abyss. The only thing that stops me is knowing that what I do can impact people's lives in a positive way. You never know how much someone can relate to your story; that everything from speaking about the death of my father and what that cost me financially, to speaking about standing up for myself in the workplace and asking for more money, can make a difference to someone somewhere.

Here are some takeaways that will help you move forward in your finances and in your life:

1. **NOTHING UNDER THE SUN IS NEW** – You will encounter many people with similar ideas to you but only you can execute on your level.

2. **THERE WILL BE TRIALS** – No one is exempt from the peaks and troughs life offers. You'll have down days, but they'll pale in comparison to the ones where you'll succeed.

3. **SELF-INVESTMENT IS KEY** – I have invested a lot into my ventures over the last few years. At more than one point I questioned if I was being foolish. People were buying houses and I felt like all I was buying was potential dreams. Little did I know one of those dreams would have me screaming my head off on one cold January day because #Merky Books wanted me to write a book about finance.

Bet on yourself every single time. No matter what the odds are, always remember they are in your favour in the end. This doesn't mean that things will always line up the way you want them to, but you will learn to take the disappointments and the disapproval of others with a pinch of salt. So, every single day that you have on this earth, make it count, give thanks, be grateful and keep betting on yourself.

GLOSSARY

APR – The term 'annual percentage rate (APR)' is the annual rate of interest charged to borrowers and paid to investors. APR is expressed as a percentage that represents the actual yearly cost of funds over the term of a loan or income earned on an investment.

APPRECIATION – Appreciation, in general terms, is an increase in the value of an asset over time. The increase can occur for a number of reasons, including increased demand or weakening supply, or as a result of changes in inflation or interest rates.

ASSET – Assets are defined as resources that help generate profit in your business and in your life. A house can be an asset as long as it goes up in value.

BUDGET – A budget is an estimation of revenue and expenses over a specified future period of time and is usually compiled and re-evaluated on a periodic basis. Budgets can be made for a person, a group of people, a business, a government, or just about anything else that makes and spends money.

CAPITAL – Capital is a term for financial assets, such as funds held in deposit accounts and/or funds obtained from special financing sources.

CREDIT – Credit is generally defined as a contractual agreement in which a borrower receives something of value now and agrees to repay the lender at a later date – generally with interest.

CREDIT CARD – A thin rectangular piece of plastic or metal issued by a bank or financial services company, that allows cardholders to borrow funds with which to pay for goods and services via merchants that accept cards for payment.

DEBIT – A debit is an accounting entry that results in either an increase in assets or a decrease in liabilities on a company's balance sheet.

DEBIT CARD – A debit card is a payment card that deducts money directly from a consumer's current account to pay for a purchase. Debit cards eliminate the need to carry cash to make purchases directly from your savings.

DEPRECIATION – Depreciation is an accounting method of allocating the cost of a tangible or physical asset over its useful life or life expectancy.

Depreciation represents how much of an asset's value has been used up. Depreciating assets helps companies earn revenue from an asset while expensing a portion of its cost each year the asset is in use. If not taken into account, it can greatly affect profits.

INVESTMENT – An investment is an asset or item acquired with the goal of generating income or appreciation. Appreciation refers to an increase in the value of an asset over time. When an individual purchases a good as an investment, the intent is not to consume the good but rather to use it in the future to create wealth. An investment always concerns the outlay of some asset today – time, money, or effort – in hopes of a greater payoff in the future.

LIABILITIES – A liability is something a person or company owes, usually a sum of money.

LIMITING BELIEF – A limiting belief is something that you tell yourself is true. It stands in the way of you and potential achievements, keeping you in a stagnant state of mind. What you believe is and isn't for you can come from what you were told about yourself growing up. This could be in the form of your culture, family members, friends at school, teachers and society.

RETURN ON INVESTMENT (ROI) – The ratio between net profit and the cost of investment. ROI tries to directly measure the amount of return on a particular investment, relative to the investment's cost. To calculate ROI, the benefit (or return) of an investment is divided by the cost of the investment. The result is expressed as a percentage or a ratio.

SCARCITY MINDSET – A scarcity mindset is defined as the belief that you are in short supply of something. Having a scarcity mindset with money can only change when you choose to see yourself and your situation differently.

*   www.investopedia.com/

everyday resources

BOOKS:

Laura Whateley, *Money* (Fourth Estate, 2018)

Emilie Bellet, *You're Not Broke You're Pre-Rich*, (Cassell, 2019)

Alex Holder, Open Up: Why Talking About Money Will Change Your Life (Serpent's Tail, 2019)

PODCASTS:

The Last Three Digits

The Which?

Planet Money

Death, Sex and Money

HELPLINES:

Citizens Advice

National Debtline

Pay Plan

Step Change

ACKNOWLEDGEMENTS

I'd like to acknowledge my book agent, Lauren, who has been so supportive of me during this process. Lauren, you believed in me when many people didn't and I have so much love for you.

Lemara, thank you so much for being incredibly patient with me, you go out of your way to make me feel like a priority.

To Bronagh, Wale and Ore, thank you so much for being in my corner. Half of the time my head is in the clouds but you all keep me grounded.

To the #Merky Books team, you are doing amazing work. I am excited for all that is to come. You are building an amazing legacy.

To my friends and family, who always support me, thank you so much for your encouraging words. I love you all deeply. I won't name all of you because I am too nervous that I'll leave someone I love out!

To everyone I've met online and offline through my work, I appreciate you more than words can describe. Every message, tweet and repost counts. If I don't say it enough, thank you!

To black women everywhere, you are the inspiration that keeps on giving. I adore you.

NOTES

NOTES

NOTES

NOTES

NOTES

NOTES

NOTES

NOTES

NOTES